A New Tune A Day
Pop Performance Pieces
for Alto Saxophone

Chord symbols for all pieces are included in the concert key for guitar or keyboard accompaniment.

Boston Music Company
part of The Music Sales Group
London/New York/Paris/Sydney/Copenhagen/Berlin/Madrid/Hong Kong/Tokyo

Contents

- **Bad Romance** *Lady Gaga* **3**
- **Brown Eyed Girl** *Van Morrison* **6**
- **Candle In The Wind** *Elton John* **9**
- **Dancing Queen** *ABBA* **12**
- **Hallelujah** *Leonard Cohen* **15**
- **I Believe I Can Fly** *R. Kelly* **18**
- **I Got You (I Feel Good)** *James Brown* **20**
- **Imagine** *John Lennon* **26**
- **(I've Had) The Time Of My Life** *Bill Medley & Jennifer Warnes* **23**
- **Love Story** *Taylor Swift* **28**
- **Man In The Mirror** *Michael Jackson* **34**
- **Someone Like You** *Adele* **31**
- **Stand By Me** *Ben E. King* **38**
- **Take A Bow** *Rihanna* **44**
- **Viva La Vida** *Coldplay* **46**
- **With A Little Help From My Friends** *The Beatles* **41**

Published by
Boston Music Company
Exclusive Distributors:
Music Sales Limited
14-15 Berners Street, London W1T 3LJ, UK.
Music Sales Corporation
257 Park Avenue South, New York, NY 10010, USA.
Music Sales Pty Limited
20 Resolution Drive, Caringbah, NSW 2229, Australia.

Order No. BM12661
ISBN: 978-1-78038-509-9

This book © Copyright 2012 Boston Music Company, a division of Music Sales Limited.
Unauthorised reproduction of any part of this publication by any means including photocopying is an infringement of copyright.

Produced by shedwork.com
Photography by Matthew Ward

Printed in the EU

Your Guarantee of Quality
As publishers, we strive to produce every book to the highest commercial standards. The music has been freshly engraved and the book has been carefully designed to minimise awkward page turns and to make playing from it a real pleasure. Throughout, the printing and binding have been planned to ensure a sturdy, attractive publication which should give years of enjoyment. If your copy fails to meet our high standards, please inform us and we will gladly replace it.

www.musicsales.com

Bad Romance

Words & Music by Stefani Germanotta & RedOne

© Copyright 2009 House Of Gaga Publishing Incorporated/
Songs Of RedOne/Sony/ATV Songs LLC, USA.
Sony/ATV Music Publishing.
All Rights Reserved. International Copyright Secured.

2

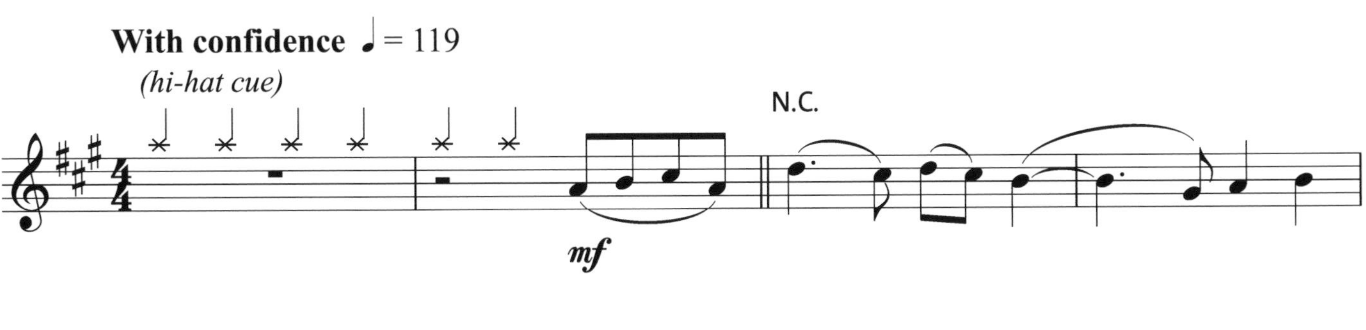
With confidence ♩ = 119
(hi-hat cue)
N.C.
mf

f

Am

Am
F
mf

Am
G
Am
F

Am
G
Am
F
Am
G
Am
F
Am
G
Am
2
Am/G
F
f energico
G
Am
C
F
G
E/G#
Am
F
G
Am
C
F
G
E/G#
Am
To Coda
1.
Am

2.
Am
f
G
Am
G
Am
mp
Am/G
Am
Am/G
mf
F
G
Am
C
F
G
E/G♯
Am
F
G
Am
C
F
G
E/G♯
N.C.
D.S. al Coda
Coda
N.C.
(solo)
mf

Brown Eyed Girl

Words & Music by Van Morrison

Brightly ♩ = 150
A♭
D♭
A♭
E♭
A♭
D♭
A♭
mf
E♭
A♭
D♭
A♭
E♭
3
A♭
D♭
A♭
E♭
A♭
D♭
A♭
E♭
D♭
E♭
3
A♭
Fm
D♭
E♭
A♭
E♭
A♭
mf
D♭
A♭
E♭
A♭

D♭ A♭ E♭ A♭
D♭ A♭ E♭ A♭
3
D♭ A♭ E♭ D♭
E♭ A♭ Fm D♭
E♭ A♭ E♭
A♭ D♭ A♭ E♭
f
A♭ D♭ A♭ E♭
A♭ 7 A♭ D♭
mf

A♭ E♭ A♭ D♭
A♭ E♭ A♭ D♭
A♭ E♭ A♭ D♭
A♭ E♭ D♭ E♭
A♭ Fm D♭ E♭
A♭ E♭
mf
A♭ D♭ A♭ E♭
f
A♭ D♭ A♭ E♭
Repeat to fade

Candle In The Wind

Words & Music by Elton John & Bernie Taupin

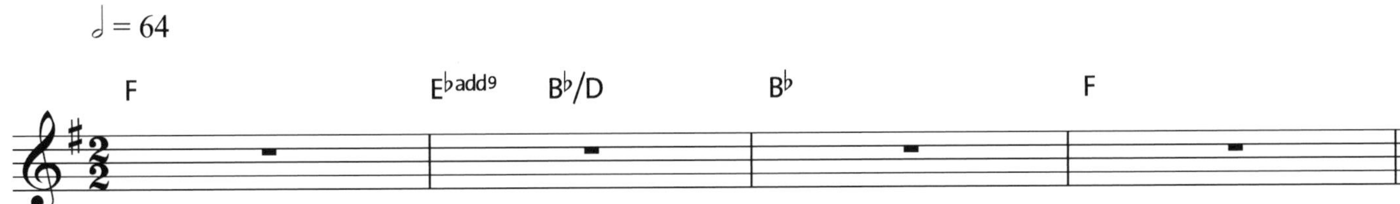

E♭
E♭add9
B♭
B♭sus4
B♭
F

E♭
E♭add9
Gm

To Coda
F
E♭
B♭/D F7sus4

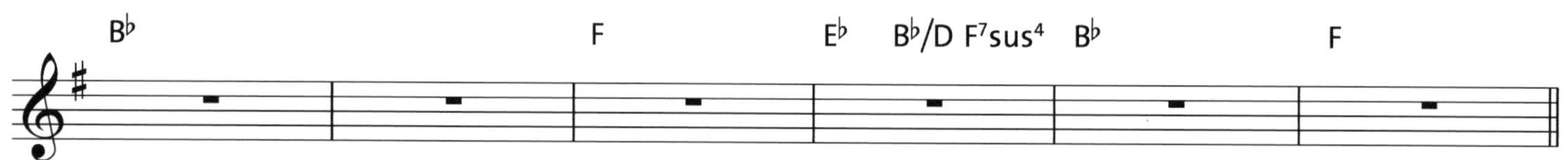
B♭
F
E♭
B♭/D F7sus4
B♭
F

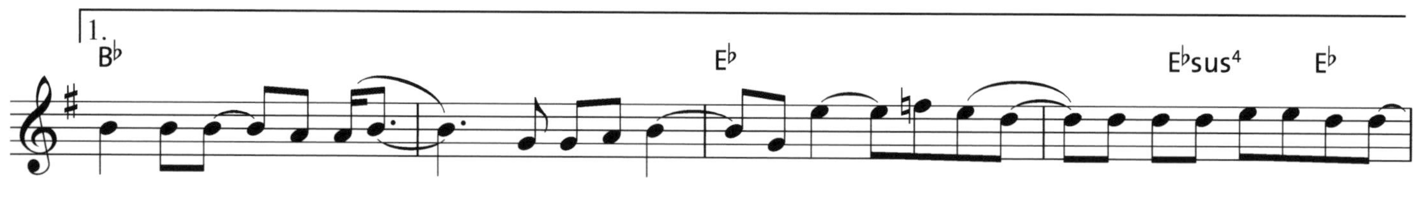
1.
B♭
E♭
E♭sus4
E♭

B♭/D
E♭

B♭
E♭
E♭add9
E♭

B♭/D
E♭
3
3
E♭add9
E♭

2.
B♭
legato
(mf)
E♭

E♭sus4
E♭
B♭/D
E♭

E♭sus4
E♭
B♭

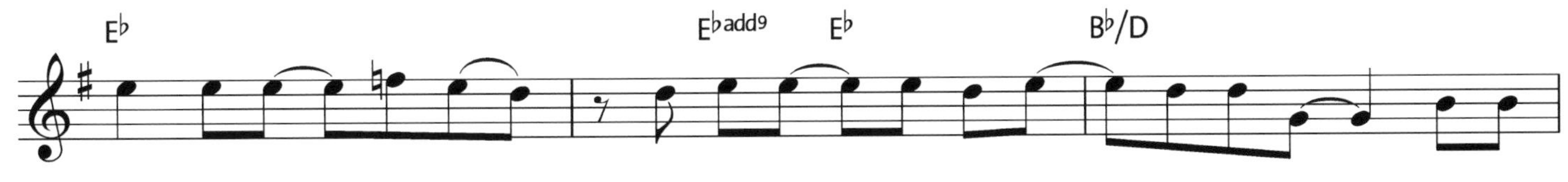
E♭
E♭add9
E♭
B♭/D

D.S. al Coda
E♭
E♭add9
E♭

Coda

B♭
Gm
F
E♭
B♭/D F7sus4 B♭

Dancing Queen

Words & Music by Benny Andersson,
Stig Anderson & Björn Ulvaeus

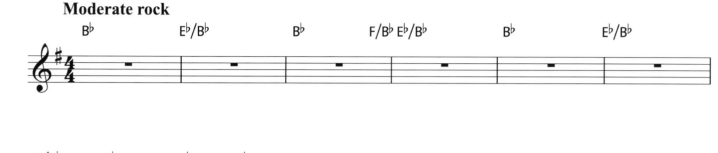

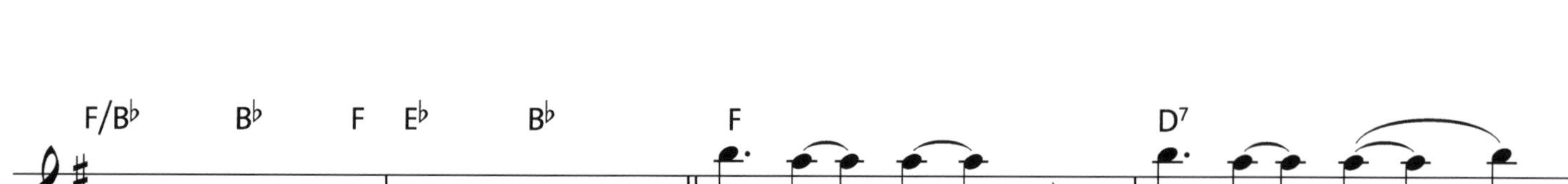

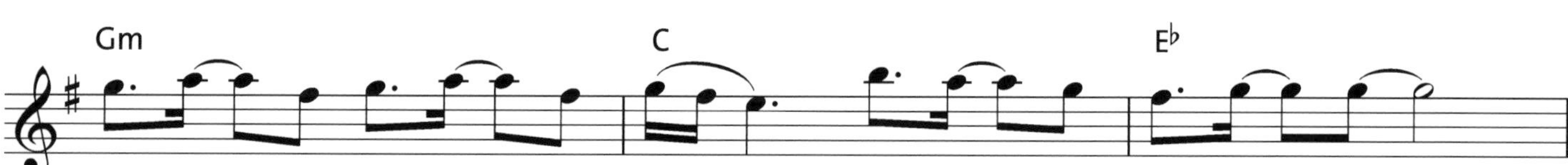

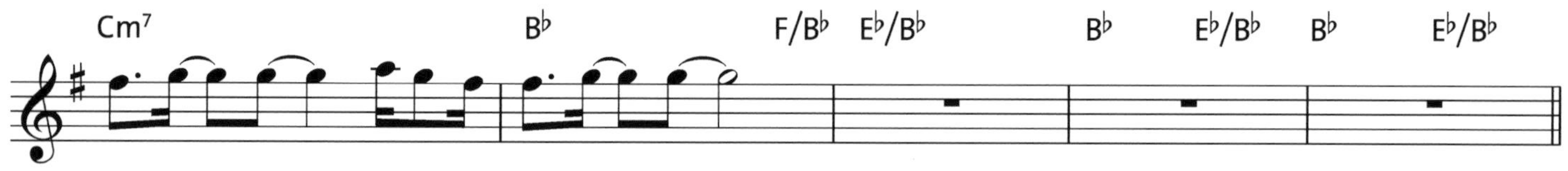

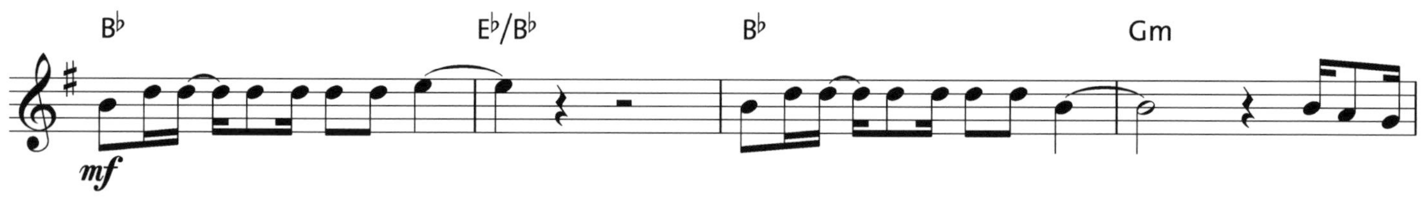

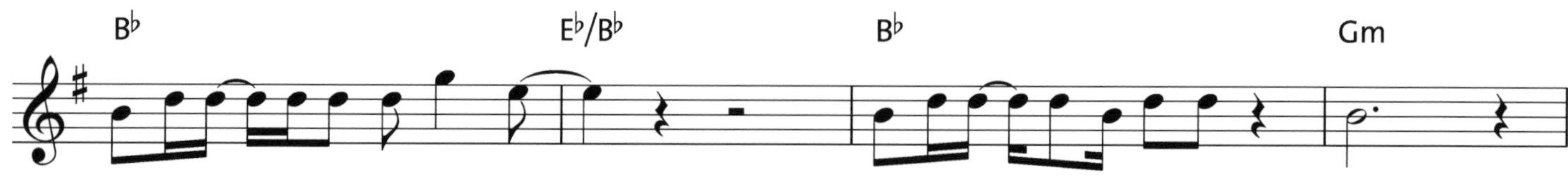

F B♭/F F B♭/F F Gm
F Gm Cm7 F7 B♭
f
E♭/B♭ B♭ F/B♭ E♭/B♭ B♭
E♭/B♭ B♭ F/G E♭/G B♭/F F
D7 Gm C7/E
E♭ Cm7 B♭
E♭/B♭ B♭ F/B♭ E♭/B♭ B♭ E♭/B♭ B♭ E♭/B♭
B♭ E♭/B♭ B♭ Gm

F B♭/F F B♭/F F Gm
F Gm Cm7 F7
f
B♭ E♭/B♭ B♭ F/B♭ E♭/B♭
B♭ E♭/B♭ B♭ F/G
E♭/G B♭/F F D7 Gm
C7/E E♭ Cm7
B♭ E♭/B♭ B♭ F/B♭ E♭/B♭ B♭
Repeat and fade
E♭/B♭ B♭ F/B♭ E♭/B♭ B♭ E♭/B♭ B♭ F/B♭

Hallelujah

Words & Music by Leonard Cohen

6

Expressively ♩. = 61
G♭
E♭m
G♭
E♭m
G♭
E♭m
mp cantabile

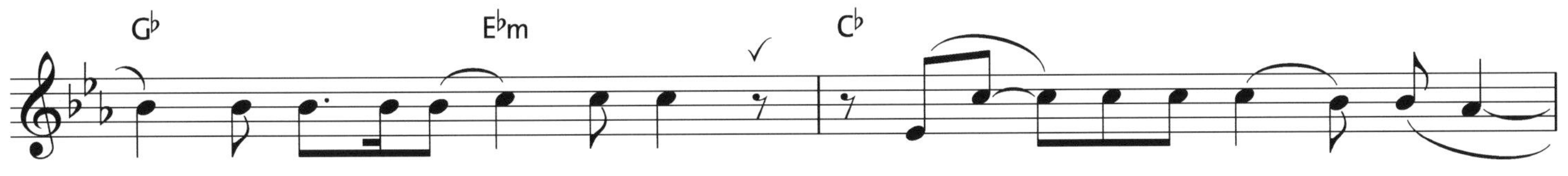
G♭
E♭m
C♭

G♭
D♭
G♭
C♭
D♭
cresc. poco a poco

E♭m
C♭
D♭
B♭7/D
f

E♭m
C♭
E♭m
mf espressivo

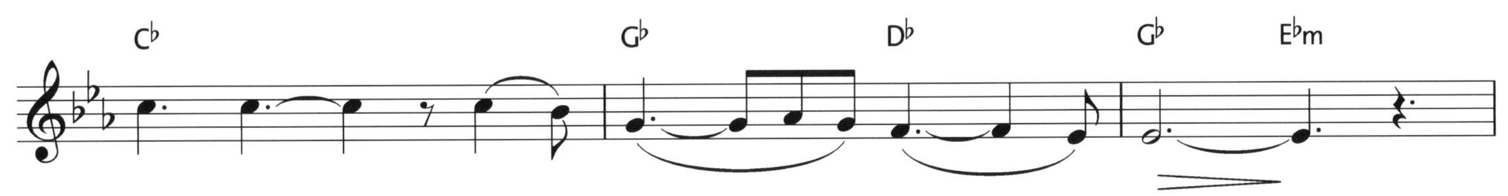
C♭
G♭
D♭
G♭
E♭m

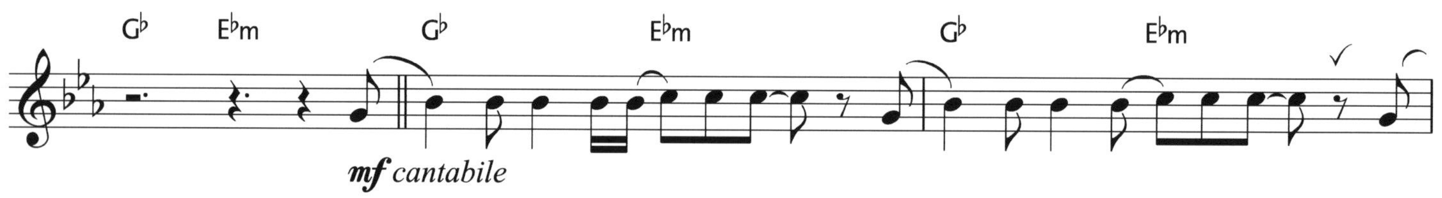
G♭
E♭m
G♭
E♭m
G♭
E♭m
mf cantabile

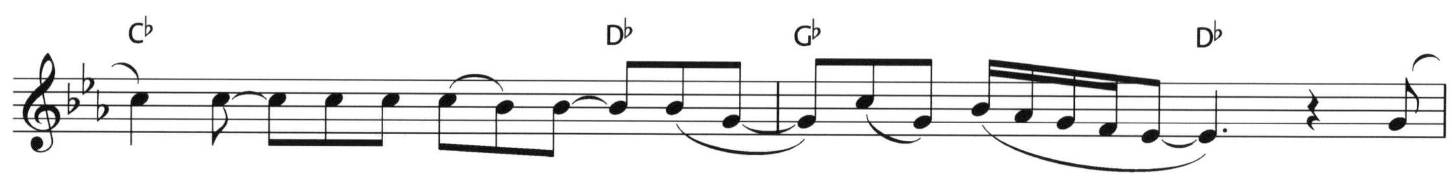
C♭
D♭
G♭
D♭

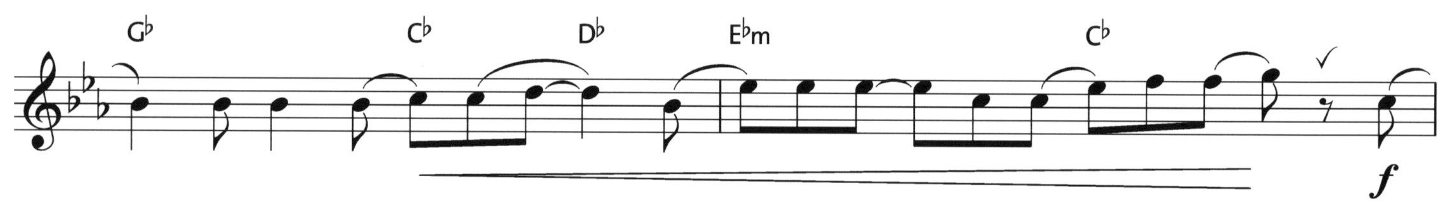
G♭
C♭
D♭
E♭m
C♭
f

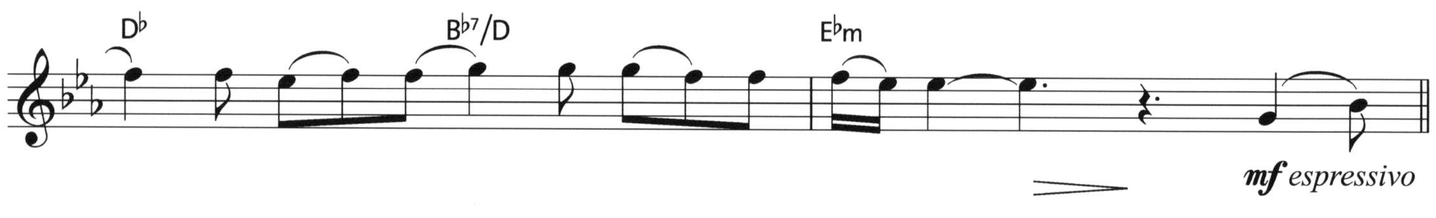
D♭
B♭7/D
E♭m
mf espressivo

C♭
E♭m
C♭

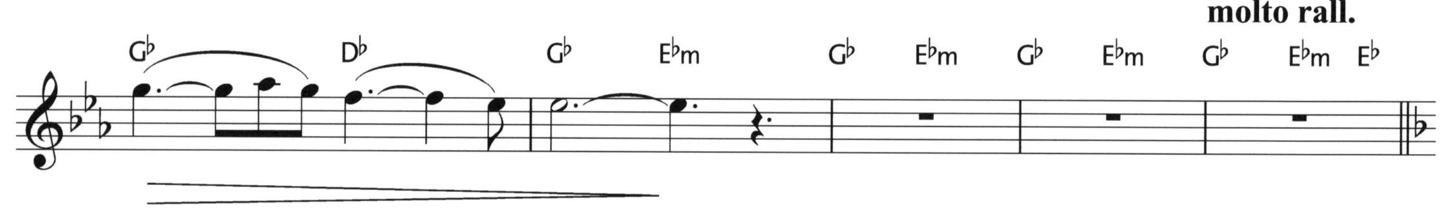
molto rall.
G♭
D♭
G♭
E♭m
G♭
E♭m
G♭
E♭m
G♭
E♭m
E♭

A tempo
A♭ Fm A♭ Fm
ff
D♭ A♭ E♭ A♭ D♭ E♭
f
Fm D♭ E♭ C7/E
Fm D♭
mf
Fm D♭ A♭ E♭
f
D♭ Fm D♭
A♭ E♭ A♭ Fm A♭ Fm
mp
rit.
D♭ Fm E♭ A♭

I Believe I Can Fly

Words & Music by R Kelly

Slow but rhythmic

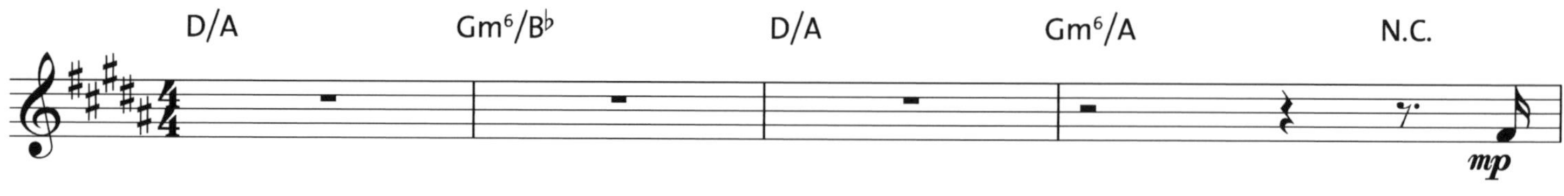

1.
D/A
Gm6/B♭
Bm7
Gmaj9/A
dim.
2.
Gm6/B♭
Bm7
Em7
D/F♯
Gmaj7/A
G7(♯5)
3
Cm7
A♭m6/B
E♭/B♭
A♭/B♭
B♭
cresc.
3
3
f
E♭
Cm7
Fm7
A♭maj7/B♭
G7/B
Cm7
A♭m6/B
E♭/B♭
A♭m6/B
E♭/B♭
rall.
A♭m6/B
E♭/B♭
A♭m6/B
E♭

8

I Got You (I Feel Good)

Words & Music by James Brown

Medium fast tempo
Tmbs.
Drums
C7

F7

C7

G7
F7
C9

C7

F7
3

C7

G7
F7
C9
3
F7
sfp
C7
F7
G7
C7
3
F7
C7
G7
F7

C9
1.
2.
C7
F7
C7
G7
F7
C9
G7
F7
C9
G7
F7
C9
poco rall.
Drums
Tmbs.
ffp

(I've Had) The Time Of My Life

Words & Music by Frankie Previte, John DeNicola & Donald Markowitz

Moderately ♩ = 109

hi-hat cue

F Dm7

mp cantabile

E♭6 F Dm7

E♭6 F Dm7

poco rit. **A tempo, with a steady beat**

E♭6 F

E♭/F

mp animato

F E♭/F

F

mf

E♭/F F

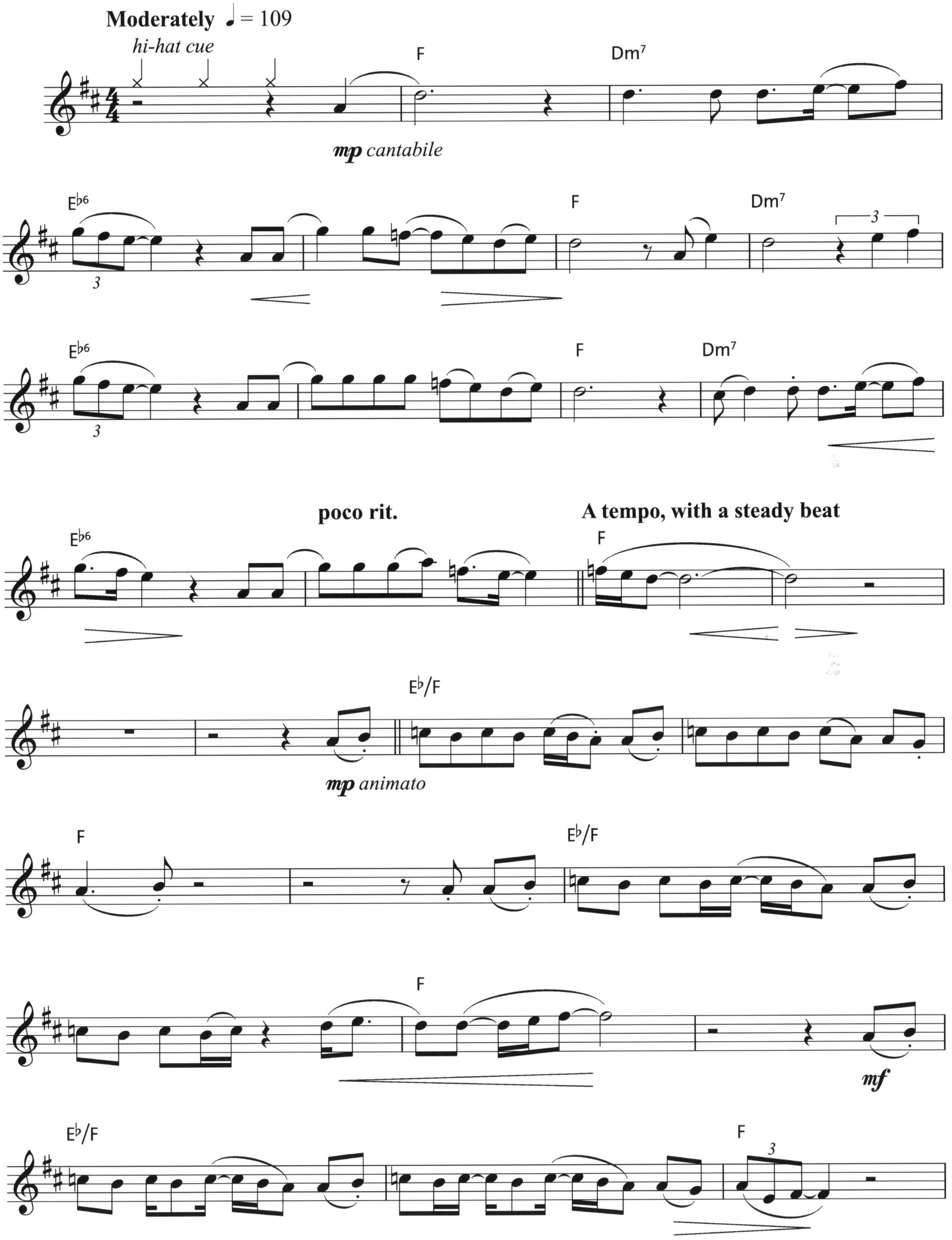

E♭/F
mf
F
𝄋
B♭
mf
mp legato
A♭
B♭
Csus4
C
B♭/C
C
F
Dm7
f
E♭
F
Dm7
To Coda
E♭
Csus4
C7
F
E♭/F
mf
F
E♭/F
F
mp animato
E♭/F
F
E♭/F
F
cresc. poco a poco

D.S. al Coda
Coda
Gm7
C
F
mf
Dm7
E♭
F
Dm7
E♭
C
F
E♭/F
Gsus4
C
F
Dm7
Instrumental break
mf
f
E♭
F
Dm7
E♭
Gm7
Gm7/C
N.C.
Softly
F
Dm7
synth./guitar/brass cue
p dolce
E♭
F
Dm7
E♭
N.C.
mf
With a heavy beat
F
Dm7
E♭
f
Repeat to fade
F
Dm7
E♭
Gm7
Gm7/C

10

Imagine

Words & Music by John Lennon

Medium slow (♩ = 76)

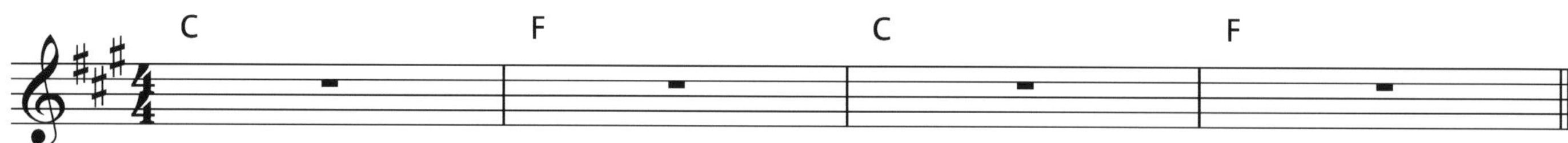

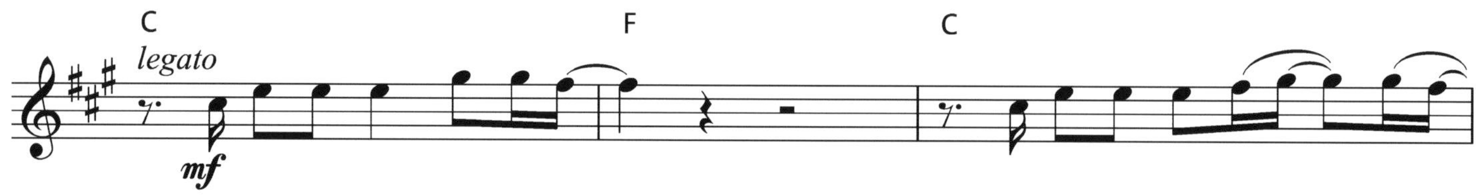

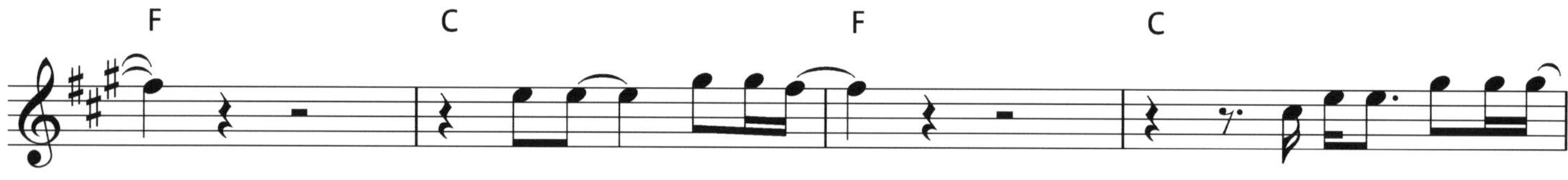

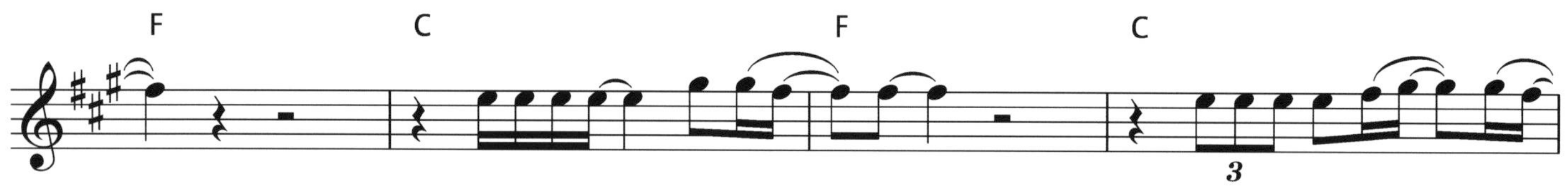

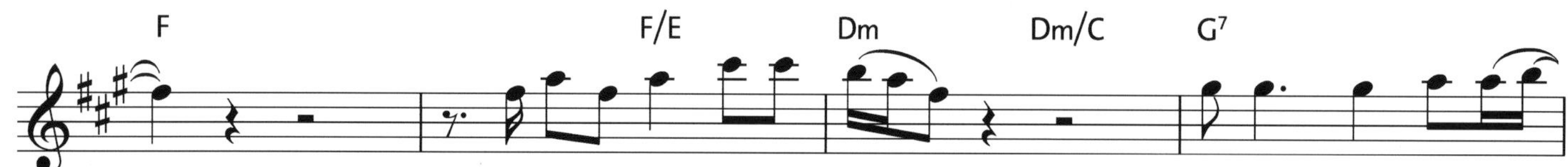

F G7 C E7 F G7
C E7 F G7 C E7 F G7
C F C
F C F C
F F/E Dm Dm/C G7
F G7 C E7
F G7 C E7 F G7
rall.
C E7 F G7 C
loco

Love Story

Words & Music by Taylor Swift

Tenderly ♩ = 119
N.C.
8
E♭add9
p dolce
A♭sus2
Cm
A♭add9
E♭add9
mp
A♭sus2
Cm
B♭
A♭
mf energico
B♭
Cm
E♭
A♭
B♭
Cm

A♭
B♭
E♭
B♭
f
Cm7
A♭
1.
B♭
E♭add9
p
mp
2.
B♭
E♭
B♭
Cm7
A♭
B♭
E♭
B♭
Cm7
A♭
B♭
mp
Cm7
A♭
E♭
B♭

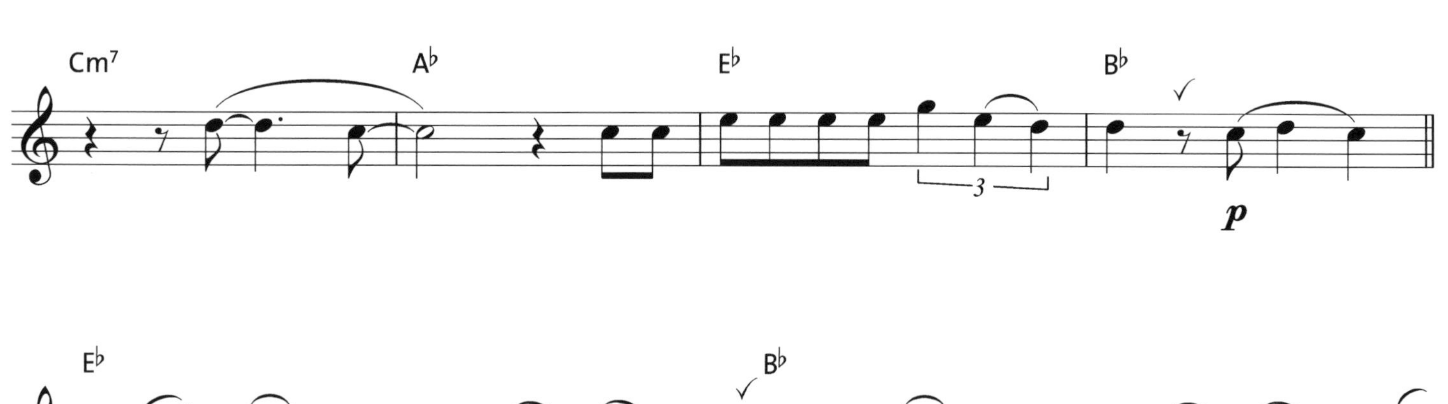
Cm7
A♭
E♭
B♭
3
p
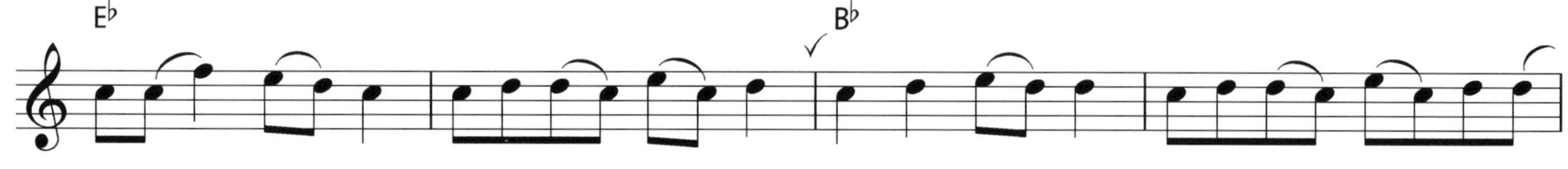
E♭
B♭
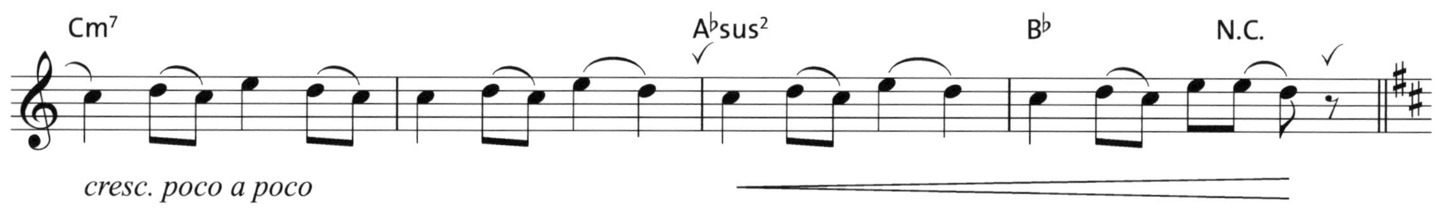
Cm7
A♭sus2
B♭
N.C.
cresc. poco a poco
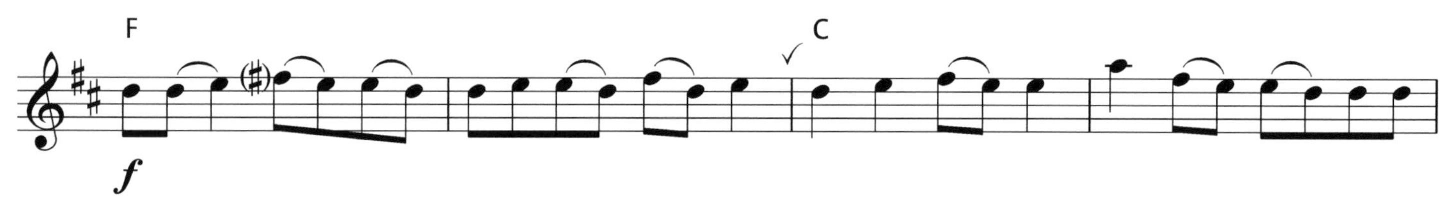
F
C
f
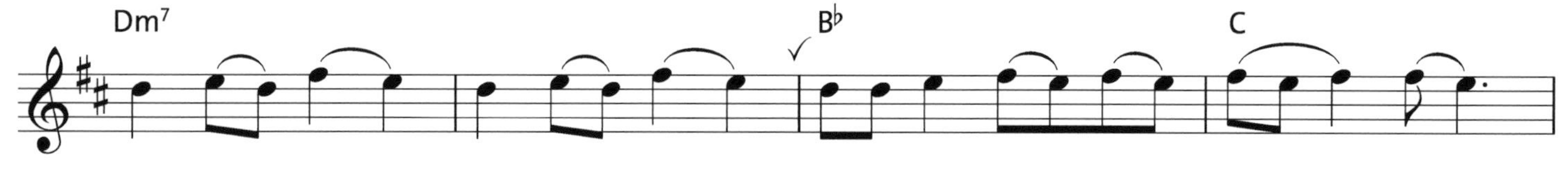
Dm7
B♭
C
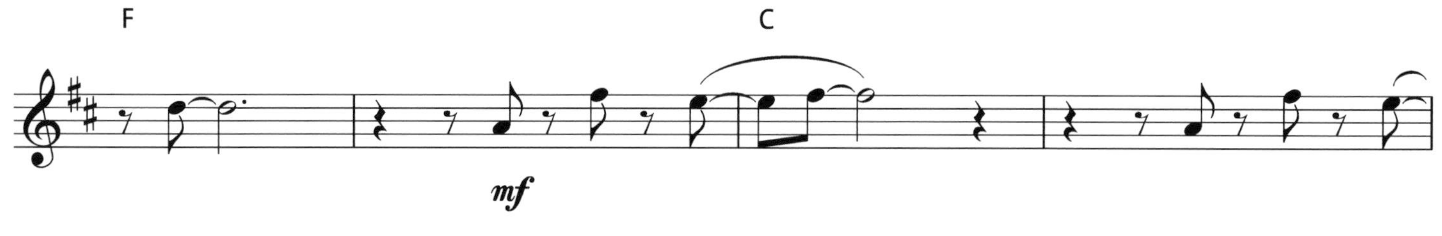
F
C
mf
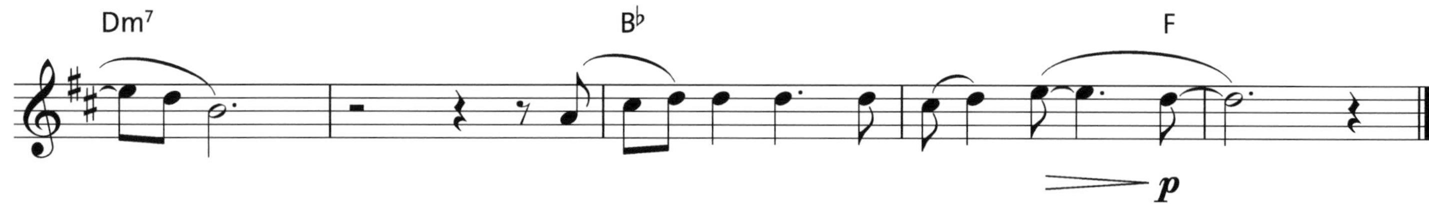
Dm7
B♭
F
p

Someone Like You

Words & Music by Adele Adkins & Daniel Wilson

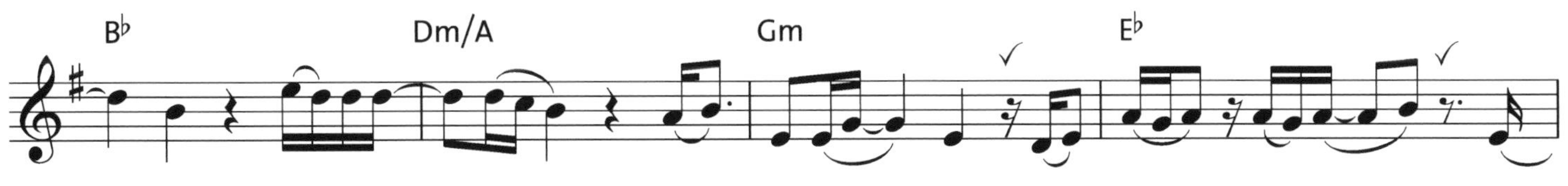

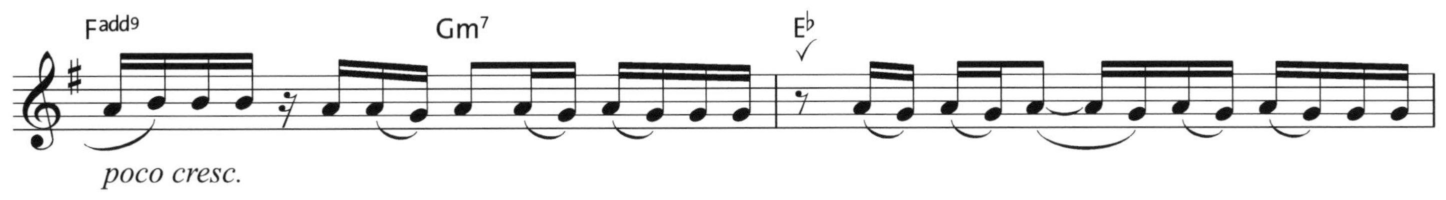

B♭ F Gm E♭ B♭ F
mf
Gm E♭ B♭ F Gm E♭
f
mf
B♭ F Gm E♭ B♭ F
Gm E♭ B♭ Dm/A Gm
mp
E♭ B♭ Dm/A
Gm E♭ Fadd9 Gm7
mp
E♭ Fadd9 Gm7
E♭ Fadd9/E♭ E♭ B♭ F
p
mf
Gm E♭ B♭ F Gm E♭

B♭ F Gm E♭ B♭ F
f mf
Gm E♭ F/C Gm/D
mp
poco rit.
a tempo
E♭5 F/C B♭/D E♭ F/E♭ B♭ F/A
mp mf
Gm E♭ B♭ F/A Gm E♭
B♭ F Gm E♭ B♭ F/A
mp
Gm E♭ B♭ F Gm E♭
f
B♭ F Gm E♭ B♭ F
Gm E♭ B♭ F Gm E♭
mf f
B♭ F Gm E♭ Fadd9/E♭ E♭maj7 E♭5 B♭5
mp

Man In The Mirror

Words & Music by Glen Ballard & Siedah Garrett

Csus4/2 F Fadd9/A B♭add9 C9sus4
f
F Fadd9/A B♭add9 C9sus4 F Fadd9/A B♭ Bm7♭5
C7♯9 F C/E Dm7
C B♭add9 C B♭/D C/E
3
F C/E Dm7 C B♭add9
mp
F C/E Dm7 C
B♭add9 Gm7
cresc. poco a poco
Fadd9/A B♭add9 Fadd9/A Gm7
Fadd9/A B♭add9 Csus4/2

F Fadd9/A B♭add9 C9sus4 F Fadd9/A B♭add9 C9sus4
f
F Fadd9/A B♭ Bm7♭5 C7♯9
F Fadd9/A B♭add9 C9sus4
f
F Fadd9/A B♭add9 C9sus4 F Fadd9/A B♭
Bm7♭5 C7♯9
F♯ F♯add9/A♯ Badd9 C♯9sus4 F♯ F♯add9/A♯ Badd9
ff
C♯9sus4 F♯ F♯add9/A♯ B Cm7♭5
C♯7(♯9)
1.
2.

F♯
C♯/E♯
D♯m7
C♯
B
C♯
F♯
C♯/E♯
D♯m7
C♯
Badd9
3
3
p
mf
f
2
mf

Stand By Me

Words & Music by Ben E. King, Jerry Leiber & Mike Stoller

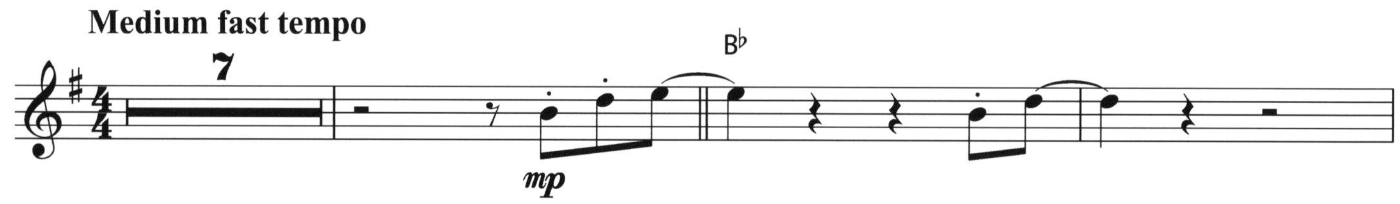

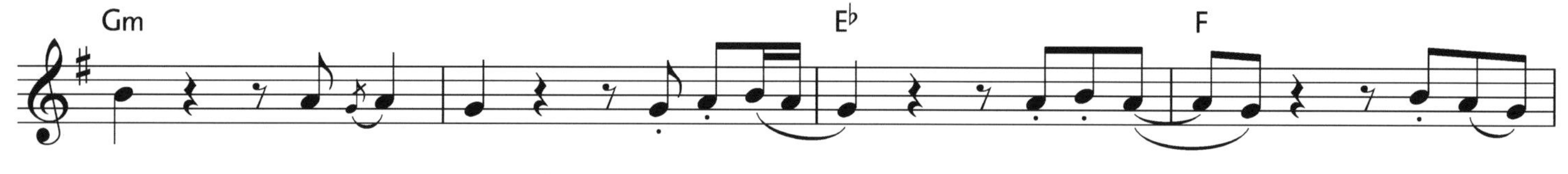

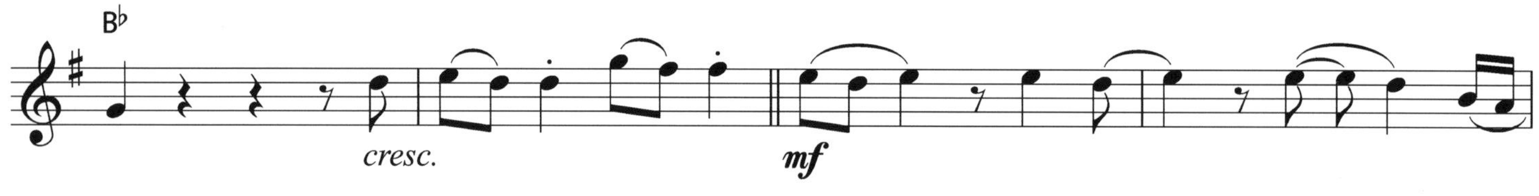

B♭
mp

Gm
E♭

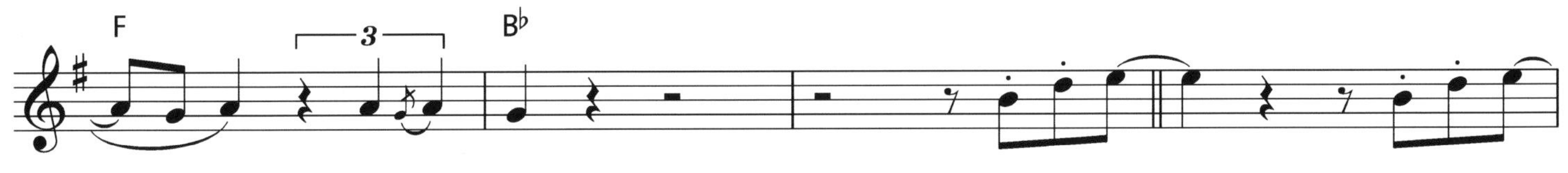
F
3
B♭

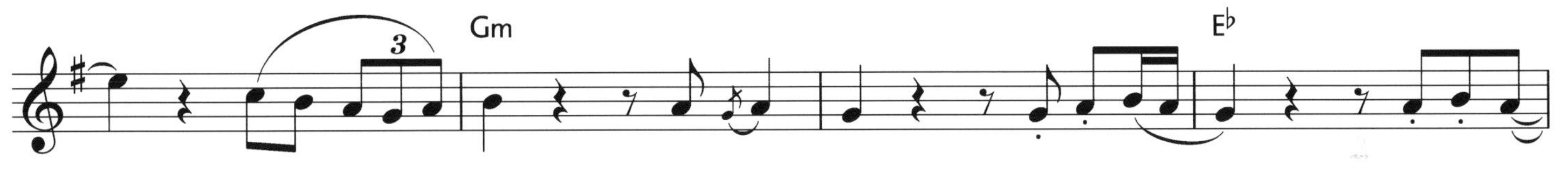
3
Gm
E♭

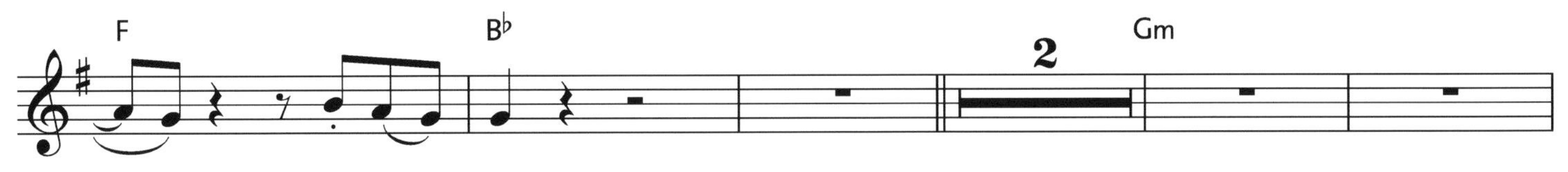
F
B♭
2
Gm

E♭
F
B♭
mp
Gm

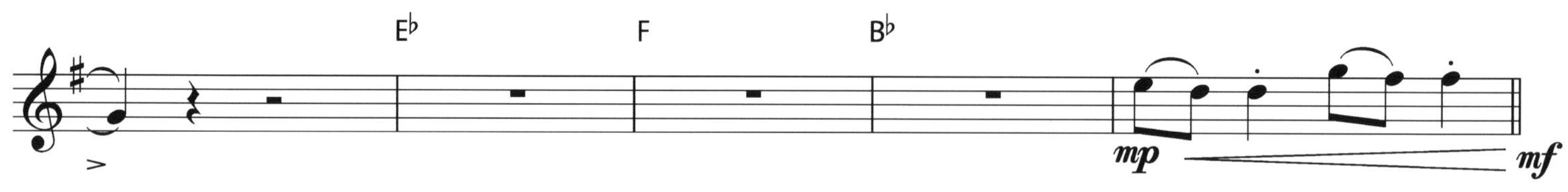
E♭
F
B♭
mp
mf
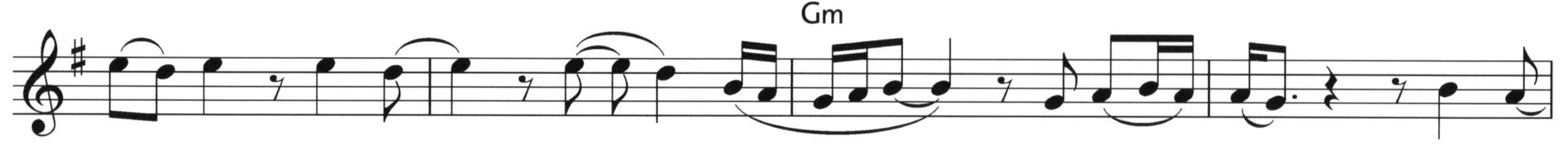
Gm

E♭
F
B♭

mf

poco rall.
Gm
E♭
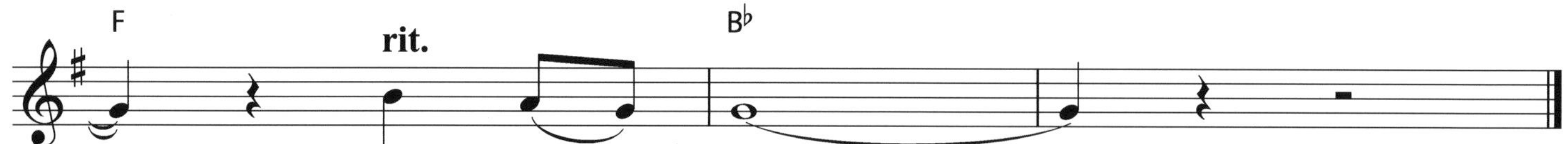
F
rit.
B♭

With A Little Help From My Friends

Words & Music by
John Lennon & Paul McCartney

15

With a relaxed lilt ♩ = 107 ♫ = ♩♪ (3)

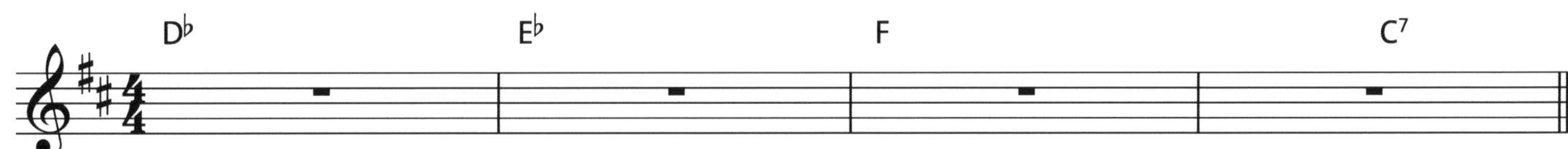

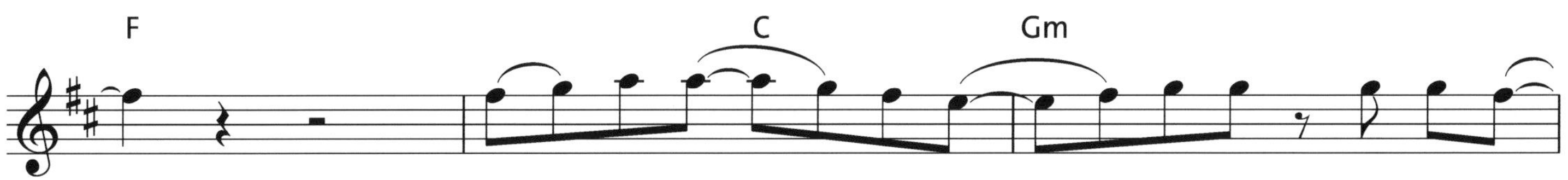

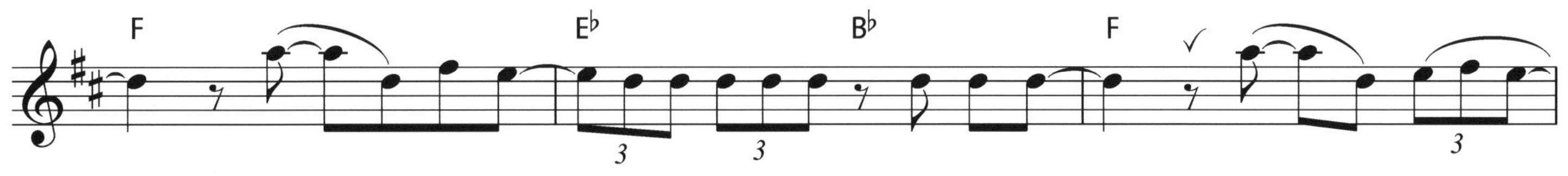

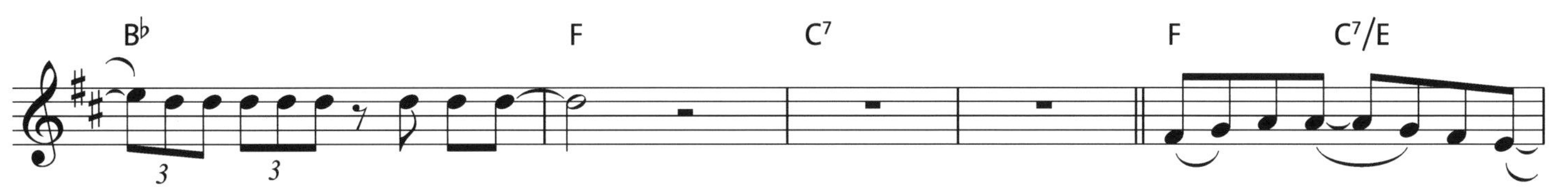

C
Gm
C7
F
E♭
B♭
F
E♭
B♭
F
B♭
F
Dm
G7
F
E♭
B♭
Dm
G7
F
E♭
B♭
F
C7/E
mf
Gm
C7
F
C
Gm
C7

F
E♭
B♭
F
E♭
B♭
F
B♭
F
Dm
G7
F
E♭
B♭
Dm
G7
F
E♭
B♭
E♭
B♭
F
E♭
B♭
F
B♭
F
E♭
B♭
D♭/A♭
B♭m6
F

16 Take A Bow

Words & Music by Mikkel Eriksen, Tor Erik Hermansen & Shaffer Smith

F C Dm B♭ F C Dm B♭
F C/E E♭sus2 F C Dm B♭
D.S. al Coda
Coda
F C E♭ E♭
mf
mf
C/B♭ C Dm7 Gm7 F/A
f
C/B♭ C Dm7 E♭
F C Dm B♭ F C/E E♭sus2
mp
mf
F C Dm7 B♭sus2 F C Dm7 B♭sus2
F C Dm7 B♭sus2 Gm7 F/A B♭6
molto rit.
B♭ F/A E♭ Gm7 F/A B♭
mp
p

17

Viva La Vida

Words & Music by Guy Berryman, Jon Buckland, Will Champion & Chris Martin

Lightly ♩ = 138

D♭maj7 E♭7 A♭ [1. Fm] [2. Fm] D♭maj7 E♭7

mp

A♭ Fm D♭maj7 E♭7

A♭ Fm D♭maj7 E♭7 A♭ [1. Fm] [2. Fm]

mf

D♭maj7 E♭7 A♭ Fm

D♭maj7 E♭7 A♭ Fm

D♭maj7 E♭7 A♭ Fm

D♭maj7 E♭7 A♭ Fm

f

D♭maj7
E♭7
A♭
Fm
To Coda
1.
mf
2.
D.S. al Coda
Coda
f
mp

CD backing tracks

1. Tuning Note

2. Bad Romance
(Germanotta/RedOne)
Sony/ATV Music Publishing (UK) Limited

3. Brown Eyed Girl
(Morrison)
Universal Music Publishing Limited

4. Candle In The Wind
(John/Taupin)
Universal/Dick James Music Limited

5. Dancing Queen
(Andersson/Anderson/Ulvaeus)
Bocu Music Limited

6. Hallelujah
(Cohen)
Sony/ATV Music Publishing (UK) Limited

7. I Believe I Can Fly
(Kelly)
Imagem Music

8. I Got You (I Feel Good)
(Brown)
Lark Music Limited

9. (I've Had) The Time Of My Life
(Previte/DeNicola/Markowitz)
Worldsong Incorporated/Sony/ATV Music Publishing (UK) Limited/
EMI Music Publishing Limited/Songs Of Pen UK

10. Imagine
(Lennon)
Lenono Music

11. Love Story
(Swift)
Sony/ATV Music Publishing (UK) Limited

12. Someone Like You
(Adkins/Wilson)
Universal Music Publishing Limited/Chrysalis Music Limited

13. Man In The Mirror
(Ballard/Garrett)
Universal/MCA Music Limited/Cherry Lane Music Limited

14. Stand By Me
(King/Leiber/Stoller)
Sony/ATV Music Publishing (UK) Limited

15. With A Little Help From My Friends
(Lennon/McCartney)
Sony/ATV Music Publishing (UK) Limited

16. Take A Bow
(Eriksen/Hermansen/Smith)
Imagem Music/EMI Music Publishing Limited/
Sony/ATV Music Publishing (UK) Limited

17. Viva La Vida
(Berryman/Buckland/Champion/Martin)
Universal Music Publishing MGB Limited

How to use the CD

The tuning note on track 1 is concert A, which sounds the same as F♯ on the alto saxophone.

After track 1, the backing tracks are listed in the order in which they appear in the book. Look for the CD symbol in the book for the relevant backing track.